DISCOVERY Gi

Fab Girls˜ Guide to

Getting Through Tough Times

Edited by Sarah Verney and Naomi Kirsten

Discovery Girls, Inc.

CALIFORNIA

Discovery Girls, Inc.
4300 Stevens Creek Blvd., Suite 190
San Jose, California 95129

Fab Girls™ Guide to Getting Through Tough Times
Copyright © 2007 Discovery Girls, Inc.

All of the stories in this collection were originally published in Discovery Girls magazine between December 2000 and June 2007. Some stories have been edited or slightly revised for inclusion in this collection. "Being Muslim in America Is Not Easy" was originally published as "We Are All Different," "Diabetes Changed My Whole Life," was originally published as "Living With Diabetes," "Drugs Changed My Cousin's Life Forever" was originally published as "A Cousin in Crisis," "I Had to Give My Pony Away" was originally published as "Silver Forever," "I'm Not Stupid" was originally published as "Learning to Live With Learning Disabilities," "I Toilet-Papered My Teacher's House" was originally published as "I Was in So Much Trouble," "My BFF Totally Rejected Me" was originally published as "A False Friendship," "My Broken Family" was originally published as "Divorce Is...Never Easy," "My Stepdad Doesn't Love Me" was originally published as "My Stepdad Doesn't Love Me Anymore," "My Mom Died" was originally published as "The Long Goodbye," and "Robbed at Gunpoint" was originally published as "Living in Fear."

Book design by Katherine Inouye Lau.

ISBN 978-1-934766-03-3

Visit Discovery Girls' web site at www.discoverygirls.com.

Printed in the United States of America.

Dedication

Dedicated to the thousands of girls who have taken the time to write to Discovery Girls magazine to share your ideas, thoughts, personal stories, and yes, even your problems. All of us who work at Discovery Girls, Inc. have been deeply touched by your letters. You are a constant source of insight and inspiration, and the reason we have created this book.

Acknowledgments

I'd like to send a special thank you to all the girls who have read Discovery Girls magazine over the years and have generously shared your thoughts, ideas, and experiences with us. Without you, there would be no Discovery Girls magazine and definitely no Discovery Girls books. I feel so very fortunate to have had the opportunity to work with my dedicated and talented staff: Julia Clause, Ashley DeGree, Naomi Kirsten, Katherine Inouye Lau, Alex Saymo, Bill Tsukuda, Sarah Verney, and interns Lyn Mehe'ula, Laura Riparbelli, and Nick Tran. Your enthusiasm and ability to keep your sense of humor while meeting insane deadlines, your willingness to work long hours, your amazing creative energy, and your insistence on always striving to get better and better have meant more to me than you will ever know—my deepest appreciation! Also, a very special thank you to artists Kathleen Uno, Bill Tsukuda, and Rhiannon Cunag for helping bring the Fab Girls to life.

Catherine Lee
PUBLISHER
DISCOVERY GIRLS

Meet the Fab Girls

Carmen

Dallas

Hi! We're Carmen and Dallas Fabrulézziano, but you can call us the Fab Girls! Why "Fab"? Well, we came up with that because Fabrulézziano isn't exactly the easiest name to say, and besides, we're totally fabulous! Ha, ha—just kidding.

We may be twins, but we're *totally* different. Carmen plans everything down to the smallest detail—from her glamorous outfits to her perfectly edited homework. She **can't live without her personal organizer**—it even helps her remember the birthdays of practically everyone in the eighth grade! Dallas, on the other hand, is too busy coming up with amazing ideas to organize anything. She's **super smart and super creative,** and you can always count on her to tell you the truth—no matter what! But even though we are so different, **we still make a great team.**

No one ever has a tough time telling us apart, and that's what's so absolutely awesome about being a Fab Girl! Even though **we're complete opposites,** we still share that special sisterly bond that makes us **the best of friends**...well, most of the time!

So, what exactly are we doing here? Discovery Girls asked us to help you through these **crazy, confusing middle-school years.** And who better to go through them with than a couple of fun Fab Girls who know exactly how you feel? We'll give it to you straight and tell you *everything* **you need to know about getting through tough times.** And remember: With the Fab Girls around, **you're never alone!**

xoxo ♡ Carmen
& Dallas

Name: Carmen

Hobbies: Acting, reading romance novels, and perfecting my chocolate-chip cookie recipe.

My biggest dream: To win an Academy Award.

I never leave home without: My planner! It's a minute-by-minute outline of my busy days—dance lessons, friends' birthdays, homework, auditions...I'd be lost without it!

Everyone knows: I'll be totally famous one day! I mean, I already had a small part in a movie...

No one knows: I'm actually very shy. When I have to give a presentation in class, I get totally nauseous.

Biggest pet peeve: People who don't RSVP. I'd love to give half my school a crash course in etiquette!

My take on Dallas: She always knows when I'm feeling down, even if I haven't said a word. She helps me think about things in completely different ways, and I'm my old self in no time!

Name: Dallas

Hobbies: Running track, photography, and playing the drums in my band. (I'm the only girl!)

My biggest dream: Yearbook editor today, world-traveling Pulitzer Prize-winning photojournalist tomorrow!

I never leave home without: Painting a tiny star under my right eye...it's my trademark!

Everyone knows: I'm a math wiz. As math team captain, I totally convinced the principal that we deserve jackets this year.

No one knows: I have a crush on the lead guitarist in my band. (But—SHHH! Don't tell!)

Biggest pet peeve: Girls who gossip and judge others. Don't get me started!

My take on Carmen: She's the most thoughtful sister! Every year on our birthday she creates a new scrapbook for me with highlights of my entire year... with doodles and pictures to match.

Contents

Introduction

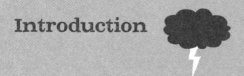

The Worst Day of My Life...and How I Survived It

An 11-year-old girl and her mom are sitting in their car when a man thrusts a gun in the window and grabs the mom's purse. The girl isn't hurt, but **for months afterward she doesn't want to leave her house...**for anything. A popular straight-A student is so mad at her newly-divorced parents that she gains 20 pounds, **pushes her friends away, and starts getting D's.** A 13-year-old starts a rumor to get back at the friend she thinks has been lying to her, only to find out she's **made a huge mistake.** The teacher's pet "honors" the teacher she adores by draping her house and yard in toilet paper...and **ends up in deep trouble.**

Tough times? You bet. Some of these stories are sad enough to bring tears to your eyes, and some might make you so angry you want to scream. But you'll find **tons of encouragement** here, too. Because as different as these stories are, there's something they all have in common: In every one, **the girl walks away stronger, smarter, and more sure of herself** than she's ever been before.

You can read these stories for comfort, for inspiration, or just to see how someone else handled **a problem you're dealing with.** They'll help you see that—no matter what you're going through—**you're not alone.** You'll meet girls who are so much like you, you'll feel like you know them. **And by the last page, you'll have a whole new way of looking at bad days** and tough times!

The Editors of Discovery Girls

Friendship

Chapter One

When You Don't Fit In

All My Friends Left Me!

In my school, the cliques have all been together since kindergarten. It's like everyone figured out who their friends should be when they were five years old and then lost interest in everyone else. You joined a group, and that was that. That never used to bother me, really, because I had my friends, too — especially my two best friends, Caitlin and Katy, who were always there for me. I'd still try to be friendly and nice to other people, and I *did* have other friends, just not close ones. Being friends with Katy and Caitlin was enough.

And then it all fell apart. We were sitting on the sidelines of our basketball game one day when Caitlin suddenly exclaimed, "Guess what?"

"What?" I replied, expecting some little surprise. Instead she said the most devastating words anyone has ever spoken to me: "I'm moving to Saudi Arabia."

"You're joking..." I saw the look on her face and quickly added, "Right?" praying silently that it was just a big joke.

Caitlin's face tensed up. "No," she replied. "I'm not. I am moving to Qatar, near Saudi Arabia. My dad's been transferred there for the next

> My best friends would be thousands of miles away by the end of June.

two years." I stared at her in disbelief, and then started to cry. Caitlin couldn't move away! What would I do without her?

Stuck at Home—Friendless

It got worse. Just a few days later I found out that Katy was also moving—to Australia! Both of my best friends would be thousands of miles away by the end of June. It was like I was a chalkboard and my friendships with Katy and Caitlin were pretty pictures that had been carefully drawn on it—and now they were being erased. Years of work were gone in an instant.

I know it was hard on both Katy and Caitlin, too. They had to leave their school, their friends—everything—and get used to new people and new places. I felt bad for them, but at least they were both going off on adventures. I was just going to be stuck at home with no friends. I couldn't help it—I felt sorriest of all for *me*.

> It was awful. Everyone had a group to hang out with—except me.

June came around so fast, and saying goodbye to Katy and Caitlin was very hard, just as I'd expected. But the rest of the summer wasn't as lonely as I'd thought it would be. Katy's mom had their computer sent by express mail, so Katy and I were able to instant message and e-mail each other right away. And sometimes I hung out with my not-so-close friends, so I wasn't totally on my own. Still, I really missed having my best friends around. I couldn't wait for school to start again—I kept hoping like crazy that there would be some new fifth grade girls that I could make friends with.

A Loner

But there wasn't even one new girl that year! It was just the same old school and the same old groups, except now I was completely on the outside. It was awful. Everyone had a group to hang out with—except me. It felt like I had just moved from outer space or something. Maybe it was even worse than being the new kid, because if I'd been new, at least some kids would have been curious about me, or they'd have been friendly because I was *new*. But since everyone already knew me, they just ignored me. I went home every night and cried. I felt so rejected! I tried hard to have a positive attitude and to be really friendly and nice, but nothing seemed to get better. In fact, the harder I tried to fit in, the more the popular kids (you know, the "pop squad") would tease me and call me a loner.

As the weeks went by, I started to think that the pop squad was right, and I was going to be stuck being a "loner" until I started middle school the next year. (Then, at least, I'd meet a lot of new kids.) But finally my mom reminded me of someone I'd overlooked.

Taking a Chance

I'd known Jill since first grade, and I'd always liked her, even though we weren't super close friends. Not only was she really nice, I realized *she* could probably use a best friend, too, since she'd been having a lot of trouble with her old "best" friends. She wasn't part of the pop squad, and I knew she wouldn't put me down for trying to be friends with her. So I decided to give it a shot.

I started hanging out with Jill every day at recess, and talking to her whenever we ran into each other. Then I invited her to

> I went home every night and cried. I felt so rejected!

spend the night at my house a couple of times. Suddenly our friendship started to blossom. Jill is so nice and so easy to talk to that pretty soon our casual conversations turned into deep conversations. We talked about *everything* —and suddenly a new piece of chalk started drawing on that chalkboard! I stopped dreading school and felt wanted and liked again.

It's been over a year now since Caitlin and Katy moved away. I'm still really close to both of them. Caitlin visited me this summer, and we even went to sleep-away camp together. And Katy is thinking about visiting for a few days this December!

Obviously, I still wish they hadn't had to move, but I also realize that there *have* been some good things about this experience. I feel more confident now about my ability to make friends, and more secure when I'm thrown into a situation without my friends by my side. I've also learned how to ignore teasing and believe in myself, and how to stay optimistic. I have definitely become stronger emotionally and spiritually. And besides all that, now I have *three* best friends—two far away, and one close by, who gives me a lift every day!

ABOUT THE AUTHOR
Lauren-Kristine, age 12, Texas

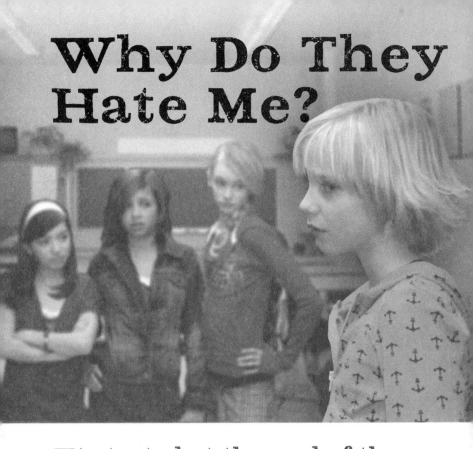

Why Do They Hate Me?

It started at the end of the semester. I'd just started taking biology. On the first day, I sat next to Jessica, who was very pretty and quite popular. Jessica's best friend was the most popular girl in seventh grade, Lindsay. As far as I know, I never did anything to make either of them dislike me, although I think Lindsay was annoyed that I took the seat next to Jessica on the first day of biology. And there was one time when Jessica got mad because she thought I'd copied her answers off a test, even though I hadn't.

I'm Not One of the Popular Kids, But...

I've never been a member of the "in" group, and I probably never will be. I've decided that's not such a bad thing, though, because sometimes it seems that a lot of the people who are in the popular crowd are real jerks.

> I was so angry and humiliated, my face felt like it was on fire!

Anyway, all of a sudden, Jessica and Lindsay started teasing me all the time. They said mean things about my hair, my clothes, and even my parents! It still hurts so much when I think about the way they talked to me, and how they embarrassed me in front of my friends.

One time, Lindsay gave me a love letter that her friend Jordan had supposedly written to me. Lindsay and her friends tried very hard to convince me that the letter was real, but I didn't buy it. Why would Jordan write a love letter to me? He was Lindsay's friend, and it was obvious by then that she hated me.

Lindsay finally admitted that the letter was phony. I felt relieved—until she turned around and told everyone in the class that I'd cried when I found out (another lie!). I was so angry and humiliated, my face felt like it was on fire! I didn't say anything, though. What could I do? I knew no one would listen if I accused pretty, popular Lindsay of lying. So I kept silent, my anger bottled up inside me.

"Loser!"

Another time, the day after we'd had a substitute teacher, I came into class and saw Lindsay, Jessica, and some of the other popular girls writing something on the black board. It said:

Hope you all liked the sub...Hehehe...
Laura Birman*

They were trying to get me in trouble! I hurried up to the board to erase it before the teacher saw it. Lindsay came up behind me and shoved me to the floor. "What the heck is your problem, brat?" she hissed. "Why did you write that on the board?"

"I didn't! That's not even how I spell my last name!" I protested, scrambling to my feet.

> Lindsay came up behind me and shoved me to the floor.

"Sure," said Jordan sarcastically. Then he called me something I can't repeat here.

"Face it, Laura," Jessica said. "You're a loser."

At that, the whole class started laughing at me. I felt like dying. To make things even worse, I knew I couldn't go to the teacher. I was having a hard time with the class, for one thing. And guess who the biology teacher's pet was? That's right—Lindsay!

A few days later, some boys told me that there was something bad written on the gym wall, and my name was on it. When I went to check it out, I could only stare in anger and disbelief. Someone had scribbled a four-letter word on the P.E. bulletin board, and signed my name! (I knew right away Lindsay had done it, because she'd spelled my name wrong—again!)

*Last name changed.

> I started to hate going to school, and my grades went down.

At this point, I decided I had to tell my parents what was going on. I knew that they would try to help, and they did. After I told them about everything that had happened, my mom decided to call Lindsay's mom. I was a little nervous about that, because I thought Lindsay would hate me for telling on her. But I also thought she'd stop harassing me, so she wouldn't get into more trouble. As far as I know, though, Lindsay didn't get into trouble at all! Her mom just said that Lindsay hadn't done anything!

Lindsay continued torturing me nearly every day. I can't list every thing that happened, but I'm sure you get the idea! I knew I didn't deserve the way she was treating me, and I knew she was a brat—I'd seen the way she treated other kids. But I couldn't help getting really depressed about it, too. I started to hate going to school, and my grades went down. My friends tried really hard to make up for all the meanness I had to put up with. They did make me feel better, but it wasn't enough to make me forget about Lindsay and her friends.

"Kick Me Hard!"

Finally, on the last day of biology—three months after all this started—things came to a head. We had a substitute that day. First Lindsay's friend, Jimmy, "accidentally" bumped me and laughed. Then he punched me and shot staples at me. When I got up to tell the substitute, everyone started laughing. I didn't know why, so I just ignored it. But then Jimmy stood up and started to write something on the board. I knew it would be something else making fun of me, so I went to erase it.

That's when the substitute said, "Uh, there's something on your back." I reached up and pulled off a paper that said, "Kick Me Hard!" The whole class got hysterical! Jordan and Jimmy were pointing at me, and everyone was laughing.

I was totally humiliated! I wanted to kick all of them, but instead, I started crying a little. I ducked my head down so no one would see, and sat down as fast as I could. As soon as class was over, I headed straight for the principal's office. I'd had enough!

Getting Help...Finally!

When I told the principal what happened, both Lindsay and Jimmy were called into his office. The principal made Jimmy write a letter of apology. Lindsay had to apologize to me in the office, but that was all. Later she told one of my friends that she got away with it and was happy.

Things did change after that, though. The school counselor talked to both of us, and put me in a different class, away from Lindsay

> As soon as class was over, I headed straight for the principal's office. I'd had enough!

and her friends. Lindsay still gives me dirty looks sometimes, but being away from her has made a big difference. I like school again, and my grades have gone back up.

So why did I have to go through all this? I don't know. I think

Lindsay is the kind of person who only cares for herself and sleeps better knowing that she has hurt someone's feelings. That still doesn't explain why she chose me to pick on, though.

Some good things have come of this experience, however. For one thing, I've learned that I can let go of my anger. I hate what Lindsay did to me, but I hate carrying anger around inside more. I don't want her to be able to do that to me, so I feel that I have to forgive her. I don't like it when other people hold grudges, so I'm not going to do it.

I've also realized that I'm a strong person. When I'm going through something difficult later on, I'll know I can handle it, because I made it through this. It's also made me aware of how important it is to be kind to other people, even someone you don't know, or don't want to be friends with. I know I never want to say something that would hurt someone—anyone—the way Lindsay and her friends hurt me. So, in some ways, as strange as it seems, I guess Lindsay has made me a better person!

ABOUT THE AUTHOR
Laura, age 12, Calif.

Chapter Two

Friendship Troubles

My BFF Totally Rejected Me

Ashley* and I weren't just pals that hung together as part of a clique—we were sincere friends, joined at the heart. You know what it's like: You share your deepest secrets and vow to stay friends forever and ever...*that* kind of friend. I had other buds, of course, but there was no one like Ashley, and I was pretty sure there never would be.

In elementary school, the thirst for popularity led some girls to care way too much about what clothes they wore and which

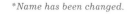

Name has been changed.

clique they should hang out with, but Ashley was never like that. Actually, that was one of the coolest things about her: Ashley saw past the glamour to who people really were on the inside. She was a serious person and a bit of a pessimist, but she was still the most loyal friend you'd ever want.

Facioscapulohumeral...

Before I tell you what happened next, there's something I should explain. I have a physical disability called (get ready— this is a mouthful!) Facioscapulohumeral muscular dystrophy, or FSHD. Imagine waking up in the morning and not being able to lift your head off your pillow. Or rolling out of bed and struggling to stand up.

> Ashley saw past the glamour to who people really were on the inside.

Imagine saying good morning to your mom without being able to move your lips, or trying to brush your teeth without being able to lift your hand to your mouth. FSHD is a constant challenge. It robs many of my muscles of the strength that most girls take for granted. Because of FSHD, I have trouble walking very far, so I use a motorized scooter to get around.

But in a weird way, FSHD can also be a gift. I often have to find creative ways to solve problems instead of just going for the obvious ones. (How would you put your sweater on if you couldn't raise your arms over your head?) It's taught me to look at things from all angles, and to really appreciate the powers of the imagination. I don't see my FSHD as a disability; it's just part of who I am. And when we were in grade school, that's all my

FSHD was to Ashley, too. She had nothing but scorn for anyone who treated me differently because of it.

Hurt and Confused

But when we got to middle school, something changed. Fabulous fashions and cool cliques closed in on us from all sides.

> But when we got to middle school, something changed.

And that's when it happened: Ashley started to avoid me at school. If I took even one feeble step in her direction, she'd dash off, tossing some dumb excuse over her shoulder. If I said hello in the hall, she wouldn't even meet my eyes. Worst of all was the fact that she always seemed to be running off to join a group of girls I'd hardly ever seen before. I'd watch them from a distance, feeling so alone. There was an awful, empty ache in the core of my heart. My "forever friend" was...gone.

And you know what was strange? Even though I missed Ashley terribly, I barely recognized her when she was with this new clique. She'd gone from a smart and confident girl to a silly, giggling, insecure gossip—overnight! I almost felt sorry for her—if she realized how she looked, she'd be horrified. But as much as I hated to admit it, even to myself, I was also kind of jealous of her new friends. She'd chosen them over me.

The Truth Comes Out

Most of the time, Ashley hung out with her new pals, but after a few weeks, she spent a little more time around me. I was so comforted to have her back, even a little, that I allowed myself to hope that she might still want to be friends. But whenever I invited her over or did something else to try to patch things up, she'd back away again. I was so confused! I guess she finally got tired of my attempts to save our friendship, because one day she told me flat-out that she just didn't want to be friends anymore. "You look weird," she snapped. From the tone of her voice, she obviously didn't care how much that would sting. "People will think I'm weird just for being around you."

That's when I knew we'd never be best friends again. I'd always thought of Ashley as someone who was too strong and confident to get sucked in by the whole middle school scene. But I was wrong—really wrong. It's one thing to say or do the right thing when it's easy—when it doesn't cost you anything. But if you're really strong, you hang in there even when it's hard, even when it hurts. You don't wound someone you supposedly care about, just because you're afraid of what people might think of *you*.

> "You look weird," Ashley snapped. "People will think I'm weird just for being around you."

In a Better World

It took a while and it hurt so much, but I finally let Ashley go. Once I did, I was able to move on and find new best friends. It wasn't easy, of course. Good friends don't just materialize out of thin air, and I couldn't help but be cautious. But when I did let myself open up, I found that there are girls out there who aren't so concerned about fashion or boys—girls who really *will* stick by me, no matter what. They're everything you could want in a friend—understanding, funny, and warm—and I treasure our friendships still.

It would be really easy to just say that Ashley was weak and wrong and leave it at that, because…well, if you ask me, she *was*. But it's also true that if the desire to be popular can make a girl like Ashley dump her best friend…well, I also think there's something wrong with the whole "system." We let the pressure to be popular have way too much power over us.

Looks shouldn't matter in a friendship, and neither should popularity. I think it's about time we changed things. If there were more girls like the friends I have now—girls confident enough not to care if someone calls them weird—maybe we could all just be ourselves, even in middle school. Wouldn't *that* be cool?

ABOUT THE AUTHOR
Aubrie, age 12, Calif.

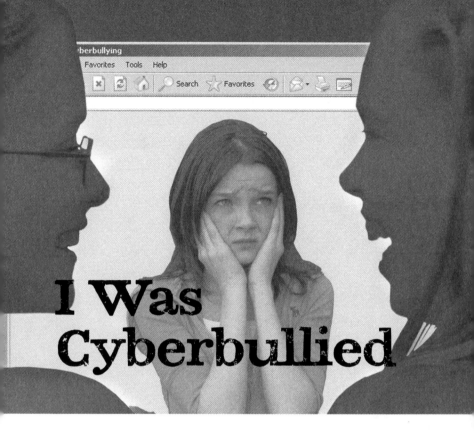

I Was Cyberbullied

I felt like I'd been kicked in the stomach. My friend Ana* had just called to tell me to check out a web site. She'd said it was bad, but I still hadn't expected *this*: "Tashana is a loser...." "Her real name is Zit Zilla...." "She's not a girl; she's an it...." I stared at the computer screen, wanting to scream. Wasn't it enough that the popular kids tortured me at school? Now it was as if they had followed me home, the one place where I felt safe. Those words were on the Internet, where my whole school could see them. Where the whole *world* could see them! I was totally humiliated.

All names, except the author's, have been changed.

When we moved earlier that year, I'd actually thought being "the new girl" would be exciting. Sure, I knew I'd miss my old friends, but I didn't think making new friends would be a problem. I'm very outgoing, and I was sure I'd get in with a fun group. Seventh grade might even be my best year ever.

> I noticed that some things were different at this school—very different.

Things started off pretty cool, too. On my very first day, a girl named Cameron introduced herself to me, and by the end of the day, I was part of her group. They reminded me of my friends back home, always laughing and having fun, and I felt totally comfortable with them. For the first few weeks, I was sure I'd been right: This *would* be my best year ever.

Popular...and Perfect?

It wasn't perfect, though. I noticed that some things were different at this school—very different. At my old school, we didn't really have "popular" and "unpopular" cliques. People liked you for who you were, not because you hung out with the "right" people. But at this school, popularity was everything, and Cameron was the most popular girl in seventh grade. People treated her like a queen, following her around and hanging onto every word she said.

Even though I hung out with them, I knew I was different from Cameron and her friends. They all looked like perfect little dolls, with beautiful skin and hair, and they all wore the latest styles. And me—well, I'm not perfect like that, but I didn't think it mattered. I thought Cameron liked me for the same reasons I liked her—because she was fun to hang out with and seemed like a loyal friend.

Before long, though, I realized that we were different in another way. Cameron and her friends were always laughing, but sometimes they were laughing *at* people. They liked making fun of people's clothes, or their looks, or even their religion! I didn't like it, but I didn't want to lose my new friends, so for a while I just let it go. But then one day Cameron and her friends were teasing this girl Ana, saying things like, "She's so skinny that no one can even see her!" I got mad and said, "Why do you guys think it's funny to put people down like that? It's so not cool!"

That's when the teasing started. Later that day I walked into a classroom and heard a group of the popu-

> Cameron and her friends were always laughing, but sometimes they were laughing *at* people.

lar kids whispering and laughing. "Look at Zit Zilla," one of them said. Then I heard "Pimple face...fish head..." And they were talking about *me*! The whole class was looking at me and laughing—all except for Ana and her friend Molly. All of a sudden, I felt sick. I wanted to run away, but I forced myself to sit at my desk and pretend there was nothing wrong. *Don't cry*, I told myself. *Just don't cry.*

Scared Silent

Just like that, I went from being Cameron's friend to her enemy. The popular kids all called me names and gossiped about me constantly. They played tricks on me, and sometimes when they passed me in the hall, they'd shove me into the lockers. It got so bad, I hated going to school. Every afternoon, I'd sit in my room and cry.

> I knew I had to speak up, even if I *was* scared.

Maybe you're wondering why I didn't just tell on them. I wanted to, but I was afraid. Sure, I'd get them in a little trouble—but wouldn't that just make them hate me more? Wouldn't they do something even worse? Besides, although I knew that what Cameron and her friends were doing was wrong, part of me kept thinking that maybe the problem was *me*. Maybe Cameron and her friends would have left me alone if I'd had perfect skin, if I'd been more like them. Maybe I *was* a loser, because why else were they doing this to me? And what if Cameron turned Ana and Molly against me, too? I felt so alone, and I was afraid I'd be even *more* alone if I spoke up.

Then I saw the web site, and suddenly, I just couldn't stand it anymore. I knew I had to speak up, even if I *was* scared. After I finished crying, I talked to my parents. And the next day, I went to the principal and told her everything.

Since then, I've learned that I wasn't alone at all. A lot of kids are victims of bullies, and a lot of girls, especially, are victims of "cyberbullies." Maybe that's because it's so easy to insult someone online—you can cut her down and never even have to see the hurt on her face. You can post embarrassing pictures or insults without admitting that you're the one doing it. For the victim, it's just as bad as being bullied in person—or maybe even worse, because the bullies can get you even when you're at home, in your own room, where you should feel safe.

I've also learned that I can make a difference

just by speaking out. We can only do something about bullying if people talk about the problem openly. Parents, teachers, and students all need to know what's going on, and kids who are being targeted need to know they're not the only ones. That's why I started telling my story to school and community groups in my town. At first, it was really hard, because I was afraid people would think I was a loser. But that wasn't what happened at all. Instead, kids told me I was brave. Some people have even called me a hero! I don't know about that, but I know I'm doing all I can to stop bullying. Think about it: Are *you*?

ABOUT THE AUTHOR
Tashana, age 13, Ontario

School Daze

You've probably read the same stories I have about being "the new girl" in school. You know the ones: The girl has trouble for the first day or so—maybe even the first week—but by the book's end, she not only has friends, she's popular!

I believed the stories, too. Then last year my family moved, so *I* was that new kid. I hated leaving the home I'd lived in since kindergarten and all my friends, but as the first day of school approached, I convinced myself that going to a new school would be a *good* thing. I was sure I'd make new friends. Of course everyone would want to be nice to the new girl, or at least *meet* her…right?

As I walked into school on the first day, my heart was pounding. All around me, kids ran up to each other, hugging and squeal-

> I drifted from one place to the next, feeling invisible.

ing. Everyone was so busy, they didn't even seem to notice me. So I made my way alone through the tight knots of people, tell-ing myself that this was typical first-day-of-school stuff. *They'll have time for me later*, I thought.

But at lunch, it was just more of the same. Most people were sit-ting in small cliques, so I sat by myself. When some kids invited me to sit with them, I was *so* relieved. Even though I didn't re-ally talk to them and no one talked to me, I still felt a lot better.

Unfortunately, it didn't last. The scene the next morning was a repeat of the day before. No one talked to me. I drifted from one place to the next, feeling invisible. Then, in class, someone finally said something.

Too Many Questions

"What's your shoe size?" a girl asked. Another kid chimed in with, "Yeah! How much do you eat?" That's how the questions began, and they didn't stop. But instead of asking my name, everyone focused on my size! I *am* short, but at my old school, no one seemed to care. I felt like a bug being examined under a magnifying glass. Maybe they weren't trying to be mean, but it hurt. Finally, I couldn't take it anymore. I ran out of the classroom, tears streaming down my cheeks. I had finally gotten what I wanted—I had been noticed—but no one saw the *real* me!

After that, no one invited me to sit with them at lunch. I tried to look busy when people walked by, but sitting alone every day hurt. At my old school, lunch with my friends was something I'd looked forward to. Now I dreaded it, and everything else about school.

> I began to think I was *meant* to be alone!

It wasn't long before I started to see myself as a loner. The weeks became months, and I wasn't even *close* to having friends. I started to feel so shy and self-conscious that I wouldn't even start up a conversation with *anyone*. As scary as the thought was, I began to believe that maybe I was *meant* to be alone! I did realize that some of the kids at my school were real snobs, and I wouldn't want to sit with them, even if they asked. But that was another problem: Was there even *one* person at this school I wanted to be my friend?

Another Chance at Friendship

Then one day I was running the mile for track when I accidentally shouldered a girl named Lauren. I thought she might get mad, but she just said it was okay. A few days later, to my surprise, Lauren started running with me! It was the first time all year someone had tried to get to know me. Before long, I started sitting with Lauren and her friends at lunch. I didn't talk much at first, because I was afraid I might say the wrong thing. It was such a relief to have friends—even just eat-lunch-together friends—that I didn't want to risk it. But as I sat there day after day, eventually I stopped worrying and started to just be myself.

That's when I realized something. Because I'd had some bad experiences, I'd thought everyone at my new school was mean, so I'd just given up on making friends. But Lauren and her friends were really nice. It had taken a long time, but I was finally starting to feel accepted.

One day, a few weeks after I started sitting with them at lunch, Lauren and a few girls were talking about going to the mall after school. "Would you like to go with us?" they asked. I said yes, trying not to act *too* excited. But just between you and me... it was one of the best days of my life!

Now I think all those stories about "the new girl" were just wrong. You don't walk into a new place and make friends overnight. It can take a long time to build trust, and sometimes you get hurt along the way. (But when you think about it...isn't that what makes friendship so special?) So if *you* end up being "the new girl" sometime soon, maybe you can learn from my experience. Be patient and hang in there. You and your friends *will* find each other. And if you're like me...they'll be friendships worth waiting for!

ABOUT THE AUTHOR
Hannah, age 12, Fla.

Family Hardship

Chapter Three

When Parents Let You Down

I'm So Disappointed in My Dad

If you met my dad, you'd probably think he was a great guy. He's fun and charming, and it's really hard not to like him. When I was little, I loved him a lot. I guess that's why it was so hard to accept the fact that he's really just a big phony.

You see, my dad has a drinking problem, and he lies, even to the people he supposedly loves. And when he drinks, he gets really mean. He and my mom used to have terrible fights, and sometimes he would hit her. Even though their fights would upset me, I didn't really understand how bad my dad was. My grandma—my dad's mom—would tell me that it was all my mom's fault that my dad acted the way he did, and I believed her.

Then, when I was eight, my mom decided to leave my dad. She was afraid of what he might do, so she went to court to get a restraining order against him. That meant he had to stay away from us, and if he didn't, he could be put in jail.

A Trial—and Jail

> Finally the police arrived and arrested him.

Then my father did something really awful, and I finally began to understand the situation. My mom and I had gone to stay with my grandma, just until we could get a place of our own. My dad got really drunk, and then showed up at my grandma's house, yelling for my mom. When my mom and I ran to the neighbors' house for help, he got violent and started throwing things and threatening to hurt my mom. Finally the police arrived and arrested him.

Because my dad had broken the restraining order, there was a trial. During the trial, my mom sent me to stay with my other grandparents in another state. When I came back, my dad was in jail, serving a two-year sentence.

During those two years I got a few letters from my dad. He told me he was sorry, and he promised he'd never act like that again. He also said he couldn't wait to see me again. I wanted so badly for it to be true that I believed everything he said. I thought he had changed, and that he'd be the dad I wanted him to be.

Let Down Again

A few days after he was released, we set up a time to meet at a restaurant. I was nervous, but I was excited, too. I thought things would be different now. Instead, he didn't even show up! I was so hurt and disappointed, I couldn't face the fact that he chose not to come. I kept making excuses for him, like he was just really late, or he didn't know exactly where we were supposed to meet. I guess I should have realized then that he'd never change, but it still didn't sink in.

For the next year my dad said he was traveling around, and then he settled down a long way from where I live. He had a new girlfriend who was really nice. She said he wasn't drinking and that everything was going well, so when they asked me to visit them, I wanted to go. I was ready to give him another chance.

At first the visit went okay, but then my dad and his girlfriend got into an argument, and he hit her. Nothing had changed—he was still the same! This time I was old enough to understand what was going on and I was really scared. Still, it was hard for me to tell my mom what had happened. Months later, I finally told her. I was glad I did, because she really helped me, and I felt much better afterwards.

> I still love my dad but I know now that I can't trust him.

I've finally realized that no matter how sincere my dad seems when he tells me he's sorry and that everything is going to be different, I can't believe him. I still love my dad but I know now that I can't trust him. He's just not going to become the kind of dad I always wanted him to be.

> I have learned that it's really important to talk about everything.

I've been through so much hurt and anger because of the way my dad has treated me and my mom. There were times when I felt like there must be something I could do to make him change, and when nothing I did or said made a difference, I got depressed. For a while, I even felt like maybe I didn't want to live anymore. It was especially difficult for me to talk to my friends about what was going on with my dad. I felt like they wouldn't understand, and that they might think it was really weird to have such major family problems.

I'm lucky, though, because my mom has made sure I've gotten lots of counseling over the last few years—both on my own and family counseling. From the family counseling my mom and I have learned that it's really important to talk about everything. I've also been in group counseling with three other girls, all with family problems. Hearing about their experiences—some a lot worse than mine—made me realize that I wasn't the only one who'd been through something like this, and that it's okay to tell people about it. Last summer, I even told one of my best friends about the things my dad has done. She was very understanding, and I'm glad I confided in her.

One thing I've realized from all this is that I don't like people to feel sorry for me. I hate it when people use things that have happened in the past as an excuse for things they do. My dad has the problem, not me, and the things my family and I have been through don't give me an excuse to say or do mean things.

Things have gotten much better for my mom and me. A year and a half ago, she remarried, so now I have a great stepdad. At the wedding, I took vows and received a wedding band along with my mom and stepdad to join us all together as one family! I also have a great cat, two dogs, not to mention a bunch of friends! So instead of thinking about my dad and all the bad things, I try to focus on the good things in my life. I don't know if I'll ever be able to completely let go of all the hurt and anger my dad has caused me, but I keep trying, and it's getting easier all the time.

If you're going through something like this, try to stay strong. Remember that you can't control anyone else's actions or change the past. You aren't alone in what you're going through, and what's happening isn't your fault. You don't have to keep it a secret! When I finally told other people about my dad, I found out that other kids had gone through similar things. Talking things out helped me a lot, and it will help you, too.

ABOUT THE AUTHOR
Diane,* age 12, Nev.

*Name has been changed.

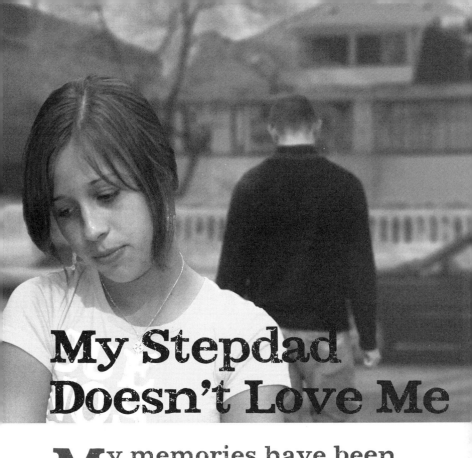

My Stepdad Doesn't Love Me

My memories have been scarred for life, thanks to the man I used to call "Dad." He was actually my stepdad, but I never really thought of him as a "step"—from as far back as I could remember, he was always just "Dad" or "Daddy." And he was a great dad, too. He'd cheer me on from the sidelines at soccer games, take me to dance lessons and swimming practice, and even help out in my classroom at school. I loved him very much, and when I was little, I *knew* I could count on him to be there forever.

My mom and stepdad divorced when I was seven. They'd been separated for a few years at that point, so the divorce didn't seem like a big deal. I was already used to him not living with us, and I didn't think the divorce would change anything. And it didn't, at first. My stepdad still picked me up every Wednesday night so we could go visit his parents—my Nanny and Grandpa—and we still spent every Sunday together. In the morning we'd go to church, and then afterwards we'd do something fun, like go to the park, or to a dog show, or to the theater to see shows like *Arthur* and *Blue's Clues*. And every Sunday night when he dropped me off, he'd tell me that he loved me and that he'd *always* love me. He was my dad, and nothing could change that...or so I thought.

> He'd tell me that he loved me and that he'd always love me. He was my dad, and nothing could change that...or so I thought.

Everything Changes

I was wrong. Not long after the divorce, things *did* start to change. My stepdad had a girlfriend, Stephanie,* a nice lady who taught piano. I really liked Stephanie, and I thought she liked me, too. She taught me how to do a cartwheel, and how to play a few notes on the piano. But as things got more serious between them, Stephanie stopped being so nice. She didn't want my stepdad to take me places on Sundays anymore, so for a while the three of us would just spend time together at his house. Then he started cancelling our plans,

All names have been changed.

saying he had things he had to do. There were even times when he just didn't show up to pick me up when he was supposed to.

My stepdad never came right out and told me that he wanted to end our visits—he just gradually pulled away more and more. He never explained why, either. I wanted to ask him, but I was too afraid. I thought he was pulling away because he was mad at me for some reason. It was so confusing, because I couldn't figure out what I'd done wrong. I wanted to ask him, but I was afraid that if I said anything, he'd get even madder and want to see me even less. Instead, I just kept quiet and tried really hard to be good so that he would still love me.

I could tell that Stephanie wanted him to pull away, and sometimes I blamed her. When I was at his house, she'd tell him not to let me do this, or not to give me that, and she wouldn't let us go places on Sundays anymore. It was pretty obvious that she didn't want me around...period. But I was more upset with *him*. Why didn't he say no to her? I was his daughter before he even knew her! Didn't he love me enough?

No Stepdaughters Allowed

My stepdad and Stephanie ended up getting married. When I first found out about the wedding, I kept asking if I could go. My stepdad would say things like, "I don't know when it will be," which really confused me. How could he not know when his own

> I kept quiet and tried to be really good so he would still love me.

wedding was? Eventually I figured out that they just didn't want me there. And once they were married, they wanted me around even less. When they had a baby, I asked to see her. The answer was no. They wouldn't even give me a picture for my scrapbook.

> I didn't know how to make him love me like a daughter again, and there was no way it would ever be like it was, no matter how much I wished it would be.

My stepdad had been paying child support for me, but he wanted to stop paying, so he and my mom ended up in court. My mom said we could also fight for my right to continue seeing him, if that was something I wanted. In some ways I did, but after thinking long and hard about it, I decided not to. I didn't know how to make him love me like a daughter again, and there was no way it would ever be like it was, no matter how much I wished it would be.

Not My Fault

Once I made the decision not to see my stepdad anymore, our relationship was over. I'd like to say I've *gotten* over it, too, but that's not really true. I think I'll always carry some of that hurt with me, like a little rock stuck in your shoe that you can't shake out. But I do understand some things better now. For one thing, I know that what happened wasn't my fault. My stepdad pushed me out of his life because he wasn't strong enough to deal with a complicated family, not because I wasn't a good enough daughter.

Right now, it's hard to imagine that I'll ever be able to think about my stepdad and not feel angry and hurt. But I also know that I'm really lucky. I have a great mom, and I know she'll always be there for me. And I *know* I'm strong, not like my stepdad. For a few years now, I've been involved in synchronized swimming, and I'm one of the top swimmers on a team that competes at the national level. All that hard work has helped to give me lots of self-confidence and taught me to believe in myself. Sometimes I feel really sad when I see other girls' dads cheering them on. But then I think, *That's his loss.* My stepdad didn't turn out to be the kind of person I needed him to be, but I'm not going to let that stop me from being the best person *I* can be.

ABOUT THE AUTHOR
Megan, age 12, Ontario

My Broken Family

Picture this: **You have a mother and father who are madly in love** (you think), a huge house, a kind, loving family, wonderful vacations, and just about anything you could ever ask for.

Then—*poof!* It all goes up in smoke. Suddenly, your parents are divorced and, well, let's just say you're not getting much of anything you want anymore. What do you do with all the anger and hurt? How do you keep your life from spinning out of control?

The Downward Spiral

I used to be a straight-A student. I got along with my parents, my teachers, other kids—everyone, really. Not that my life was perfect. I'd always liked to eat, and sometimes, I'd eat just because I felt like eating, not because I was hungry. So I was a little bit overweight, but only a little. It wasn't a huge problem.

And then my parents split up. I knew they had been fighting a lot, but I thought it was just something they were going through. I thought they'd work it out. But a divorce? How could they?

Right away, everything changed. My dad moved out of my parents' bedroom and into the guest room down-

> My grades slid to C's, and I started getting into trouble.

stairs. We stopped doing things as a family. If my parents had to be at some event together, they avoided each other like poison. I'd watch them from across the room, wishing they would talk to each other. Or I'd try to figure out a way to get them back together. I kept thinking, *If I could somehow do or say the right thing, we'd be a real family again.*

It didn't happen. Instead, my dad moved out of the house entirely, and then my mom and I had to move, too. I hated my new neighborhood, and I hated hearing that there was no money for the things I'd always taken for granted.

My anger grew. My grades slid to C's, and I started getting into trouble. I was rude to people, even people I knew really cared about me. Did I feel bad about it? Definitely. I didn't want to make everyone miserable, but I had so much anger and pain inside. Spreading my misery around was one way to let it out. It made me feel better, at least for a little while.

> The angrier I got, the more I ate.

So did eating. The angrier I got, the more I ate. Instead of being a little heavy, I became seriously overweight. Kids at school began to pick on me, and girls I thought were my friends abandoned me. I'd come home and stare into the mirror, crying and thinking I looked hideous.

A Surprising Realization

Then something strange happened. It was at my bat mitzvah. My parents had been separated for some time by then, and I was still angry and miserable inside. Still, I'd imagined that day would be different somehow. I'd always pictured my parents together at the bat mitzvah. They'd stand side by side, beaming at me, proud of what I had accomplished.

It didn't happen like that, though. At the reception, my parents stayed as far away from each other as possible. Their bad feelings toward each other were crystal clear to me now. I was so disappointed I felt like crying.

But the way they acted made me realize something. If my parents couldn't get together for something as important as this—and I knew my bat mitzvah was important to both of them—they'd never be able to. They were never going to be the way they used to be. They'd chosen to be apart, and there was nothing I could do to change that.

You might think that realization would have made me feel worse than ever, and in a way, it did. But in another way, it set me free, because the next thing I realized was that, although I couldn't change their lives, I could change mine. I *could* accept this new life and find a way to make the best of it. To do that, I obviously had to find more positive ways of releasing my pain. The only question was, *how*?

Finding an Answer

For me, the answer was to control my eating and start exercising. I realized that if I liked the way I looked, I'd feel better about myself and my life, too.

The first weight-loss program I tried was a disaster, but then I found one that really worked. It was reasonable, so sticking with it didn't seem that difficult. Even better, I signed up for a synchronized swimming class and dance lessons. They gave me a way to work off some of my anger, and they also took my mind off the negative things happening at home. I began to feel cheery and full of life when I was swimming—as if anything were possible!

> I *could* accept this new life and find more positive ways of releasing my pain.

Eventually, I dropped 20 pounds. I got along better with my teachers, and my grades improved. I found a smile on my face more often. As I began to feel better about myself, I stopped caring so much when kids teased me. I realized I had friends, real friends who had stood by me when things were really bad. I learned to just ignore the kids who'd been mean to me.

Of course, I still have to live with the changes my parents' divorce brought to my life, and I still don't like many of them. To be perfectly honest, I still feel angry sometimes. The holidays are especially tough for me. At a time when families are supposed to be so close, I end up torn in two directions. Some days, I think my parents were selfish to divorce. I feel like they should have stayed together for me, even if their marriage wasn't perfect.

But mostly, I've gotten more comfortable with the situation over time. I can even see that some good things came from the divorce. For one thing, I don't have to listen to my parents fighting anymore! But more important, because of all I've been through, I found a strength inside myself I never knew I had.

I know now that I'm strong enough to rely on myself when other people let me down. And I know that I can change my life when I need to. I've come to realize that I don't have to let my anger and disappointment spill over into everything and practically ruin my life. I can't change the fact that my parents are divorced, but I *can* change my reaction to it. And that's made all the difference.

ABOUT THE AUTHOR
Torrie, age 13, Ariz.

Chapter Four

Tough Times for Families

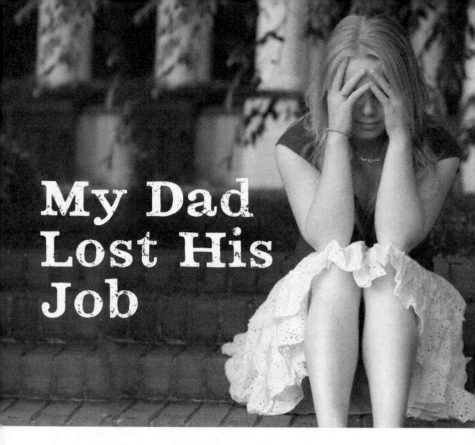

My Dad Lost His Job

My family has moved a lot, so I've gotten pretty used to walking into a new school and making new friends. It doesn't even bother me that much—I always know I'll feel at home in the new place after a few months. But about a year ago, when I was 11, we moved again, and that time it was completely different. We'd only been in our latest home for eight months, so when my parents told my brothers and me that we were moving yet again—and right away—I was really surprised. But the reason we were moving was the biggest shock of all: My father had lost his job.

And that wasn't even the worst of it. My father had been fired because he had cancer. So now he had a terrible illness and no job. In fact, neither of my parents could work for a while, since my mom had to give up her job in order to be with my dad while he got the treatment he needed to get well. I couldn't imagine how we would manage—what if neither of my parents could find work again? Suddenly the security I'd totally taken for granted was just gone. It was so scary.

> Suddenly the security I'd totally taken for granted was just gone.

Turned Upside-Down

While my parents went to another city for my dad's medical care and to look for work, my younger brothers and I moved into my grandparents' apartment. Between starting at a new school in the middle of the year, being away from our parents, and worrying about the future, our lives were turned completely upside down. My youngest brother, who was only four at the time, was too young to really understand what was happening. But I took it very hard, and so did my 10-year-old brother Luke.

Luke and I have always been close, but after my parents left he shut out everyone, even me. I missed my parents so much, and not being able to feel close to my brother made it even worse. And on top of everything else, I was worried about him. He had started to develop facial "tics"—jerky little twitches of the muscles in his face. Even though I understood that they were caused by all the fear and anger he was feeling, the change in him scared me even more.

I wanted to keep my faith in my parents, I really did. I knew they were counting on us, and I didn't want to disappoint them.

> I cried a lot, and for the first time in my life, I started to hate school.

But I was so sad and angry that for a long time, I just did the easiest thing: I gave in to all those crushing feelings. I cried a lot, and for the first time in my life, I started to hate school. I didn't even try to make friends. *Why bother?* I thought. We'd just be leaving again soon, and they'd never become *real* friends, anyway. How could anyone possibly understand what I was going through? I kept to myself so much in the first month that most people decided I was selfish and unfriendly.

Friends for Hard Times

Luckily, there were two girls at my school who reached out to me. They asked me questions about my life. Why had I moved to Florida? Why was I living with my grandparents? Where were my parents? When I finally started to talk, it was such a relief to share all the pain and fear I'd been holding inside. And Melissa and Nicole really listened. They seemed to understand what I was going through, even though I'd been convinced no one would. Their caring warmed me up so much that pretty soon I had a whole group of friends. I still wanted my family back to normal, but I stopped hating school, and my problems became much easier to bear.

I'm happy to say that life is back to normal now. It wasn't easy and it didn't go by fast, but my dad did get better, and my parents eventually found work and a new home for us. The day we all moved back in together was one of the happiest days of my life. A few months later, Luke's tics gradually disappeared, too, and our relationship returned to normal.

All of which goes to show you that when one door closes forever, at the other end of the hallway a window opens, allowing the sunshine to make its way back in. I was so wrong to think that I wouldn't make close, lasting friendships during those hard times. I met the best friends I'll ever have, and I know now that they'll always be in my heart.

I also learned something really important during those hard times: You don't have to go through the bad times alone. If you shut yourself off, it just makes everything more painful. When all you want to do is crawl into a dark hole and be left alone, reaching out may seem like the hardest thing to do—but it's also the very best way to help yourself. I know that now, and the next time trouble comes around, I won't forget it.

ABOUT THE AUTHOR
Janine, age 12, Calif.

Drugs Changed My Cousin's Life Forever

My cousin Mike* and I have always been very close. He and his mom live in our neighborhood, and our families are close, too, so we've grown up spending a lot of time together. And even though he's six years older than I am, we've always had a special connection. Mike is like the older brother I never had, but even better, because we've never had to share a house or parents!

A few years ago, we were at a family party at my house, and I got bored and went outside. Mike came out after me and asked

*Name has been changed.

if I wanted to play basketball. We had a good time, just the two of us. The next day, he called to ask if I wanted to hang out with him again. All we did was watch TV, but we really enjoyed being with each other. There were a lot of days like that, and we became as close as anyone could imagine.

Hurtful Words

But when Mike was 16 and I was 10, things started to change. It seemed like he was distancing himself from everyone in our family, including me. At the time, he'd started high school and was working at a grocery store, too, so it didn't seem that surprising that we didn't see him as often as before. But what was surprising was the way he acted. When I saw him on the street, he was very cold. He'd glare at me, or just ignore me. Sometimes it felt like he was just being mean for no reason. One time, at another family gathering, I asked him if he wanted to play basketball. "Leave me alone, Ashlee," was all he said. I know that doesn't sound so bad, but it really hurt. Still, I thought maybe he was just having a bad day, so I tried to let it go. When I saw him a couple of days later, I smiled at him, but all I got in return was that glare. It broke my heart, but I did my best to shrug it off.

> Then one night my dad suddenly rushed out of the house and was gone for a long time.

Then one night my dad suddenly rushed out of the house and was gone for a long time. The next day was Mother's Day—a big deal at my house!—but my dad didn't come home until late. I couldn't figure out what was going on, but finally my parents sat me down and explained everything. My dad had gone to help my aunt. She had just found out that Mike was on drugs, and had been for over a year.

I felt like I was in a horrible nightmare. At first I didn't want to believe it. Mike was my cousin, not a drug addict! I felt so shocked. It was the worst thing I have ever gone through in my life, and I cried for hours and hours.

So Confused

It was hard to go on as if everything was okay, but I knew that I had to. So I went to school and did my homework and everything else I usually do, even though I had so many feelings crashing around inside me that I felt confused and miserable most of the time.

Sometimes all I could think about was how worried I was. At the time, my class had been learning about how drugs can really hurt your body, and I was scared that whatever Mike was taking would kill him. But mostly, I was angry—angrier than I had ever been in my life. I had looked up to Mike and believed in him so much, and now, suddenly, I couldn't anymore. And to make it even worse, he didn't want to get help—not at first, anyway. I couldn't understand how he could hurt his family—

> I started to think I hated Mike, and that I'd never be able to forgive him.

my family—like that, not to mention himself. I'd hear my mom and dad talking about Mike sometimes, and it just crushed me to know that he was breaking their hearts, too. I started to think I hated him, and that I'd never be able to forgive him. But I also felt like I should still love him, and forgive him, too.

Luckily, I was able to talk to my mom and dad about what was going on inside me. My dad helped me realize that I did still

> I finally started to feel like I had my cousin back.

love Mike, and that the reason I was so worried was precisely because I loved him so much. And my mom helped me realize that loving someone includes forgiving them, even when they do something terrible.

I didn't see Mike for a long time. First he went away to a drug treatment home for troubled teens, and then he went to live with his dad. Finally he started coming to his mom's house on the weekends. He seemed happier and more relaxed than he had been before. Then, after Christmas break, he came back home to live with his mom. One night, we all played Scrabble, and he was laughing and enjoying himself, like he used to. I finally started to feel like I had my cousin back.

Getting Better

It's summer now, and Mike and I are spending a lot of time together again. We have a great time, and it makes me really happy. I know this has been a long, hard road for him, and it's not over yet. He's still in therapy with a doctor, and he's working again, and going to summer school so he can graduate. I'm sure that's not easy, but I'm also sure he knows now how much I love him (as does the rest of my family) and that we will always be here for him.

I know Mike has learned a lot from this experience, and he's not the only one. I have, too. I've learned how important it is to stand by the people you love when they're in trouble. The drugs tore my family apart, but that tear has been sewn back up, thanks to a lot of love and time spent together.

I've also learned not to judge someone on one mistake, or on one part of his or her life. I realized that the problems Mike had were just one small part of who he is, not the whole picture. In spite of his addiction, I think he's one of the greatest people I know. If you learn one thing from my story, I hope it will be to love and support the people you care about all the time—even when they make mistakes.

ABOUT THE AUTHOR
Ashlee, age 12, Texas

SECTION THREE

Loss

Chapter Five

Living in Fear

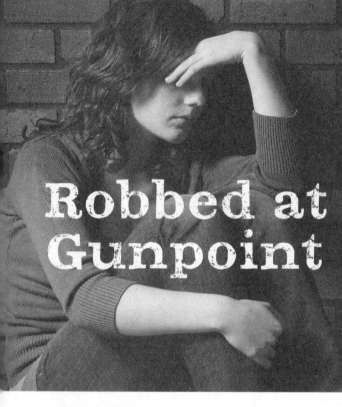

Robbed at Gunpoint

The day started like most Saturdays. My mom and I ate breakfast and then drove to a performing arts center for my rehearsal. I was in the chorus of the opera *Hansel and Gretel*. It was just a small part, but the chance to work with professionals was a dream come true.

When we arrived at the center, we couldn't find a parking space, so we parked on a side street around the corner. Since we were early, we sat in the car and read for a few minutes. Then I opened the door to get out.

The Unthinkable Happens

Suddenly there was a man in front of me, blocking my way and leaning into the car. He was filthy, and he smelled terrible. He put his hand on my leg, pinning me to the seat, and pointed a gun at my mom. I screamed—I've never been so scared in my life! I was so terrified I almost felt like it was happening to someone else. This couldn't really be happening to *me*!

I didn't know what the man wanted. I was too shocked and scared to even think, but my mom reacted quickly. She threw her purse at him, and he grabbed it and took off on his bike.

We just sat there, shaking, for a few minutes. Then my mom used her cell phone to call 911. I felt better—saf-

> But the next day I wasn't fine—not at all.

er—after the police officer got there, but even so, I didn't want to get out of the car at first. But by the time we'd answered all of his questions, I was feeling a lot calmer, so I decided to go to the rehearsal in spite of what had happened. I thought I was fine.

But the next day I wasn't fine—not at all. Suddenly I was afraid to get in a car, especially my mom's car. The fear was so bad, I didn't want to go anywhere, not to school or even to rehearsal, which I loved. When I *had* to go somewhere, I was a wreck. I'd get really nervous whenever the car stopped, even if was just for a red light. Even though I knew better, I couldn't stop thinking that someone would try to get into the car the minute it stopped moving. The thief hadn't just stolen my mom's purse, he'd also taken something from me—something much more valuable than money or credit cards. He'd stolen my sense of well-being.

My parents tried to help. They kept saying, "It's okay. No one got hurt. It's over." They couldn't understand that I really *did* get hurt. I just didn't have any scratches or bruises or broken bones, because all my wounds were on the inside.

Fear Takes Over

As time went by, things got worse instead of better. I started to be afraid of anyone who looked at all like that guy. I knew that wasn't fair, but I couldn't help it. I was living with so much fear that I just couldn't be rational about it. My emotions were in control, not my mind.

> I just didn't have any scratches or bruises or broken bones, because all my wounds were on the inside.

Finally my parents realized that I needed help, and they found a counselor for me to talk to. It felt good to talk to someone about what had happened. I could tell the counselor how scared I was, and even that I'd been really mad at my mom. She hadn't done *anything* that day—she'd just given the guy her purse! I guess part of me wanted her to be Superwoman, to fight the guy off somehow. But after talking to the counselor I realized that my mom actually *had* done exactly the right thing. If she hadn't given the guy what he wanted, we might have gotten hurt.

I also realized that I was letting this man have too much control over my life. I could take that power away from him if I really wanted to. Maybe we couldn't get my mom's purse back, but I could steal *me* back from him.

Facing It

So that's exactly what I did. Of course, it didn't happen over-night, and it wasn't easy. The only way to overcome my fears was to face them—and that meant doing the things that scared me most. My parents helped by insisting that I confront difficult situations, and by going through them with me. I also got so tired of missing out on things I really wanted to do that I just refused to let my fear stop me anymore.

It's been over a year now, and things are much better. Don't get me wrong—I still get scared sometimes, and I still find myself misjudging someone just because he looks like that man. But now I recognize what's happening, and I deal with it. I don't live in fear anymore, and I don't let some stranger have power over me.

I believe that things happen for a reason.

I learned a lot from this. For one thing, I'm much more aware of my surroundings than I used to be, and that's a good thing. But even better, I learned a lot about myself. I know now that I am a strong person and a survivor. And I'm sure of one thing: I won't ever let anyone take me away from *me* ever again.

ABOUT THE AUTHOR
Morgan, age 11, Fla.

Being Muslim in America Is Not Easy

September 11, 2001, is a day that will stay with me forever. I was so shocked and sad when I found out what had happened. My family and I cried for the people who had lost loved ones—all those children whose fathers or mothers weren't coming home anymore!— and the ones who suffered so much. I felt so scared.

And then, to make things even worse, I found out that some people thought my culture and my people were to blame. You see, my parents are from Afghanistan, and we are Muslims—just like the hijackers claimed to be.

We Are Americans, Too

When the attacks first happened, we heard that some people were taking revenge against Muslims—*any* Muslims—because the hijackers were Muslims, too. People told us to put an American flag on our car, because otherwise the windows might be smashed. I was afraid to go

> We hadn't hurt anyone, yet people were blaming us for what happened!

out, and afraid that someone might hurt my family. So for the first month we mostly stayed in our house, except when we went to school. It was very scary, and it felt so unfair, because we are Americans, too. We hadn't hurt anyone—we would never hurt anyone—and yet people were blaming us for what had happened!

That wasn't the first time I'd felt like people didn't understand what my religion and my culture are about. I used to go to a public school, and I was the only Muslim girl there. Because I wear a *hijab* (a head scarf), I got teased a lot. I wanted to make friends so badly, but I never did. Sometimes I tried to talk to the other kids or join their games, but they wouldn't give me a chance. One girl was especially mean. She would call me names like "baldy," and say that I wore the scarf because I had no hair, and even push me around.

"Islam" Means "Peace"

I know, of course, that all Americans aren't like the ones who wanted to smash in our car windows, and all girls aren't like the one who pushed me around in school. Still, I think maybe these things would not have happened at all if people understood more about Islam, my religion. (To be Muslim means that your religion is Islam—just like if you are a Catholic, your religion is Catholicism.) I would like other girls to know that the word *islam* means "peace" in Arabic, and that our most important law is that you must not kill someone. For a Muslim, that is the worst thing you can do. I think

> I would like girls to know that *islam* means "peace" in Arabic.

if people understood that, they would know that the hijackers were not true Muslims; they were just terrorists. And I would like you to know enough about my religion and my culture, so that the next time you see a Muslim girl wearing a hijab, maybe you'll smile at her and think, *I know about that*, and maybe, *She's not so different from me*.

In many ways, Islam is a lot like Christianity and Judaism. We believe that there is one God (we call him Allah) who created everything in the world, and that God gave us certain laws that we must follow. Also, we believe that if you obey God in this life, when you die you will go to heaven, where everyone has everything they want—whatever makes them happy.

But Islam is different from other religions, too. Muslims must pray five times a day, for one thing. Our prayers do not take long—just a few minutes—but we must pray at certain times every day, no matter what else we are doing. We also believe that women and girls should not show their beauty when they are out in public or when there are men around. That is why Islamic girls wear a hijab. We believe that women and girls should be very modest. We wear loose clothing, so that we are not showing off our bodies. Also, we don't do some of the things that other American girls do, like go to movies (because they might have inappropriate scenes), or to sleepovers if there are males in the house (like a friend's brother or father), or to boy-girl parties.

Proud to Be Muslim

I know that all of this may seem a little strange to you, but I am very proud of my culture and my religion. It makes me feel happy and good inside to honor God by following his laws. I do not want to see movies or do things that go against the values I have been brought up with. I used to obey God's laws because my parents told me what was right and what was wrong, but now I am old enough to know for myself. (And when it comes to parties, I think girls have more fun with their girlfriends, where they can relax and just be themselves, instead of worrying about some boy!)

And even though my life is different from yours, I bet we have a lot in common, too. I love to talk and giggle with my friends, and play soccer and basketball and spend time with my family and work hard in school and go shopping, and…well, you get the idea!

It's been several months since September 11 happened, and I'm not afraid anymore. But I'll always remember how it felt to

> And even though my life is different from yours, I bet we have a lot in common, too.

be judged on looks alone, by people who didn't know anything about me or my family. Even when I was little, I knew it was wrong to be mean to other people just because they were "different." But because of everything that has happened, I understand even more now how important it is for us to respect other people and their religions.

We all need to love and accept each other, as God teaches us, because we are all human beings, even if we are not exactly the same. I also know that we are very lucky to live in a country where everyone is able to worship the way they want and get a good education and live peacefully. I am proud to be a good Muslim—and an American, too.

ABOUT THE AUTHOR
Shakiba, age 12, Calif.

Chapter Six

Losing Someone You Love

I Had to Give My Pony Away

Silver was beautiful. The first time I saw her, I couldn't take my eyes off her, and I couldn't believe she was really mine. I had a *pony*, my very own Shetland pony! I was so excited, I could hardly stand it. She was the best birthday present any five-year-old ever got!

Within days, Silver became my best friend. I loved brushing her shaggy silver coat, and I loved riding her. I'd even run to her when I was upset about something. I'd stand on the fence of Silver's corral and talk to her as if she were a person. Somehow, she always made me feel better.

Silver made me laugh a lot, too. She was sneaky, always stealing food from the other horses when no one was looking. Sometimes I'd catch her in the act, but then she'd look at me as if to say, "Who, me?" and instead of getting mad, I'd just giggle. I'd laugh at the way she was so stubborn sometimes, too. She'd absolutely refuse to do something I wanted her to do—until I waved a carrot or an apple under her nose. She just couldn't resist a good bribe.

> A couple of years after I got Silver, she started to limp.

The Bad News

A couple of years after I got Silver, she started to limp. We weren't too worried at first, but after a few days my parents decided we'd better have the vet look at her. That's when we got the bad news: Silver had Cushing's Syndrome, a disease that sometimes causes a horse's hooves to grow abnormally. Imagine if your toenails were separated from the nail beds, and you had to walk on them—it would be really painful, right? That's sort of what Cushing's Syndrome did to Silver. Our vet said she probably felt like she was stepping on razor blades. She also told us that there's no cure for Cushing's Syndrome—at least not yet—and it can be very hard to treat.

I felt like someone had hit me in the face with a rock. Silver—my best friend—was suffering, and there was no way we could make her well again! But then the vet explained that there was some good news, too. Even though Cushing Syndrome doesn't have a cure, there are things you can do to keep the horse from suffering. When I heard that, I silently promised myself—and Silver—that I'd do whatever I could for her.

I tried, and so did my mom and dad. Following the vet's instructions, we changed Silver's feed and gave her tons of medicine. But taking care of her feet was more difficult. Even a healthy horse needs to have its hooves trimmed by an experienced horse shoer. For a horse with Cushing's Syndrome, the job is extra hard to do, and it needs to be done a lot more often. We had Silver's hooves trimmed as often as we could, but it still wasn't quite enough.

Still, Silver got better for a while. But then she got worse again. We went through a few months like that. She'd get better, then worse, then better, and then worse again. Finally my parents told me that I had to make a decision, since it wasn't fair to let Silver suffer like that. We could either put her to sleep, they said, or we could give her to my mom's cousin, Sharon. Sharon is a former professional horse shoer, so she would be able to trim Silver's hooves as often as she needed. Also, Sharon was able to get a special kind of low-protein hay that isn't available where we live, and that's better for horses with Cushing's Syndrome.

Doing the Right Thing

I hated the thought of saying goodbye to Silver. Of course, I didn't want her to be in pain, and I wanted her to have a good life. But I also felt really sorry for myself. I

> I felt like I was losing my best friend, because I *was*.

felt like I was losing my best friend, because I *was*. It was awful. There wasn't really any choice, though—I knew what I had to do—so I told my mom to tell Sharon that she was getting a new pony.

I'll never forget the day we took Silver to Sharon. After the long drive, I took Silver out of the trailer so I could say goodbye. I talked to her softly, petted her neck, and hugged her. Then I got back in our truck and just sat there, biting my lip and blinking really hard. I managed to hold back my tears until Sharon drove away, but then I couldn't stop them any longer. I cried all the way home.

I was still missing Silver a lot a few months later, when a letter arrived from Sharon. Inside, there were some pictures of Silver. When she was really sick, her coat had gotten very thick and matted, but in the pictures, she looked like her old self again. Her coat was all smooth and silvery and beautiful.

At that moment, I knew without a doubt that I'd done the right thing for Silver, even though it hurt so much to give her up. Someday I hope to have a horse of my own again. But no matter what, I know I'll never have another horse or pony like Silver. She'll always be special to me. I'll never forget you, Silver.

ABOUT THE AUTHOR
Lilly, age 11, Calif.

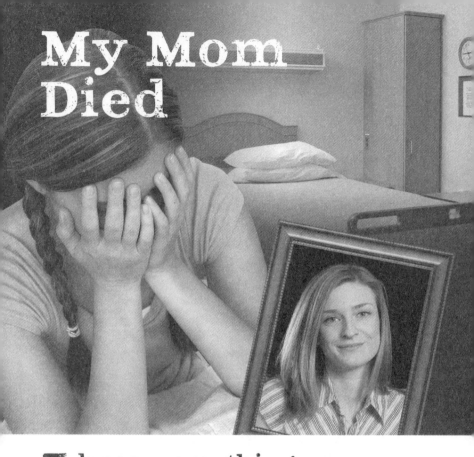

My Mom Died

I knew something was wrong. My little brother and I were eating dinner when we heard our parents whispering in the other room. We went into the kitchen and saw that our parents were crying. I asked what was wrong, and my mom said that she had cancer again. When I was four, my mom had been sick, but she'd had a special treatment and the cancer went away. We all thought that was the end of it. Since I was really young at the time, I didn't really know what cancer was anyway. All I knew was that my mom had gotten better, and that was all that mattered.

But even six years later, I still didn't really know what cancer meant for my mom. And for much of that year, I didn't even know how terrible things were. I mean, nothing bad could happen to my mom, right? It turned out that my friend's mom and one of my mom's friends were also diagnosed with cancer, so it seemed like lots of people were going through the same thing. *Maybe it isn't really that bad*, I thought. *Maybe it's normal, even.*

> As I turned 11, I began to realize how serious my mom's illness was.

Waiting for a Cure

Together, my mom and her friends went through chemotherapy—a treatment for cancer that involves taking very strong medication. The chemotherapy drugs help kill the cancer, but they can also make all your hair fall out, so for months my mom and her friends wore wigs, scarves, and hats. (My brother and I loved trying on my mom's wigs.) Eventually all her hair started growing back, and the cancer seemed to be backing off.

Around that time, my friend's mom was cured—just like that. I was happy for my friend, but I was also secretly jealous. I wanted *my* mom to get better, too, but she was still left to fight.

As I turned 11, I began to realize how serious my mom's illness was. My parents were traveling all over the country—and even to Mexico—to find a cure, and it was getting harder for my mom to walk. When she did, she limped. It wasn't long before she was in bed all the time, too weak to get up.

One day I came home from school and couldn't find anybody. I finally found my brother, who said that our mom was in the hospital. When my dad came home, he took us there. I was happy to be going to see my mom, but that changed when I actually saw her. She could barely breathe or drink on her own—it just took too much effort. It really hurt to see her like that.

> One day I came home from school and couldn't find anybody.

Home...but Not Better

After about a week in the hospital, my mom came home. I was so happy because that obviously meant she was better. But she wasn't. She still couldn't walk or breathe well. Then one night as I said goodnight and hugged her, she said, "I'm going to try to live to be around with you, but if I'm not, just know that you are going to do fine in life."

I told her that of course she was going to be around for me, and that I loved her too much for her to not be there!

The next day I went to school with butterflies in my stomach. I just knew my mom had gotten worse over night. During second period, the principal came to get me and started explaining that my mom's time was up. It was time for me to go home and say goodbye.

Back at home, my mom didn't look like herself. She wasn't talking right and her eyes were rolled back into her head. I started to cry very hard and took her hand. She was having trouble making words come out right, but I heard her say my name and that she loved me. I told her I loved her too. Then she made a weird sound and I ran away. I knew that she was gone.

I cried and cried. Then some people came and took her away.

Life Without My Mom

I didn't go to school for the rest of the week. At her memorial service, people talked about how loving my mom was. On the piano, I played two songs by Enya, my mom's favorite composer. Playing for my mom and hearing everyone say such nice things about her made me feel so good that for a while, I forgot to be sad.

I loved my mom very much, and still do. The day she died, I closed my eyes and tried to picture my life without her. I couldn't. In a month, I would turn 13—I'd be a teenager—and I needed my mom for that!

But as a little time has passed, I've realized that when I just think about her, I feel confident and strong. I recently went skiing for the first time, and as I started going down a really steep hill, I was frightened. But then, all of a sudden, I wasn't scared anymore. I couldn't help but think my mom had something to do with that.

And I know that throughout my life, no matter how difficult things are, I'll feel that way. I think my

> The day my mom died, I closed my eyes and tried to picture my life without her. I couldn't.

mom is now my guardian angel, always watching over me and

giving me the strength to be brave and happy—the way she wants me to be.

Whenever I *do* feel bad, I like to think about the time my mom and I went snorkeling in Hawaii. As the clear water swirled around us, I saw some big fish and sharp coral. I was scared, but my mom took my hand and said that the big fish weren't going to hurt me.

Since she was brave enough to go underwater, I knew I was, too. Everything was blue, yellow, and orange, and the sun streamed through the water in beams. Life was all around us. It was just the fish, my mom, and me. I felt really close to her, and safe. After an hour, I'd forgotten all about my fear, and didn't want to leave. I just wanted to stay there, with my mom, forever.

ABOUT THE AUTHOR
Mackenzie, age 13, Ore.

Overcoming Dark Times

Chapter Seven

Making Amends

I Was So Wrong!

Carrie* and I were going to be best friends, I was sure of it.

My old best friend had moved away, and Carrie was new to our school. Not only was she really pretty, but she was fun to be around, too. Within days, she was part of our group.

But I felt like it was hard to get close to Carrie. Whenever I tried talking about personal stuff, she'd change the subject. Everything always had to be light and fun, which got kind of frustrating. Still, I never really got mad at her...until my birthday party.

All names, including the author's, have been changed.

By then, Carrie and I were hanging out every day during school, and we IM-ed every night. But I hardly ever saw her outside of school, and I still couldn't really talk to her. I'd tried inviting her to sleep over a few times, thinking we'd get closer that way, but there was always some reason she couldn't do it. Then I invited Carrie to my birthday sleepover, and she said she'd be there. Finally, we were actually going to hang out outside of school!

Rejected?

But an hour before the party, she sent me an IM claiming that her mom was sick and couldn't drive her over. I told her my dad could come get her, but she said she had to stay with her little brother. That's when I started to get mad. How could her brother need a babysitter? He was 11! I was sure she was just ditching me.

> I was sure she was just ditching me.

It got worse. A couple of days later, my friend Allie said someone she knew had seen Carrie and another girl at the mall on the night of my party. I couldn't believe it! I was good enough to be her friend at school, but that was all!

I was so mad, I started ignoring Carrie at school, and I refused to answer her IM-s asking me what was wrong. Finally Allie told her why I was mad, and Carrie wrote me a long note. She said that her mom really *was* sick, and that she had a good reason for being at the mall, but that it was hard to explain. I didn't believe her for a minute. What other reason could there be?

I felt betrayed, and I wanted to get back at Carrie for hurting me. And—I admit it—I was jealous, too. It seemed like Carrie had everything—she was pretty, she got good grades, and everyone liked her (especially the boys!). It wasn't fair.

Getting Back at Carrie

So I started a rumor. I was IM-ing Allie one night, and the next thing I knew, I'd told her that Carrie had told me she'd gotten in trouble at her old school for stealing money from her teacher's desk. Within a day, the rumor was all over school, and I heard that Carrie was crying in the bathroom at lunchtime. I felt a twinge of guilt, but I also thought she kind of deserved it. Then, that night, Carrie IM-ed me. "Y do u h8 me?"

> I felt a twinge of guilt, but I also thought she kind of deserved it.

"y did u ditch me on my bday?"

"didnt....its complic8ed," she answered.

A few seconds later my cell phone rang. "It wasn't what you think," she said. "My mom *was* sick and Scott really did need me."

"Oh, sure," I said sarcastically. "That's why you were at the mall with your real friends."

"That was my cousin, Abby," Carrie said.

"Whatever," I said, and I was just about to hang up when Carrie started talking, her voice so low it was hard to hear her. "My mom's an alcoholic," she said. "She's getting better, but when I came home from school that day, I could tell she'd been drinking. It's just my mom and Scott and me, so I had to call my aunt and uncle. They probably would have brought me to the party, but I didn't want to leave Scott. The only reason we went to the mall was that my uncle thought it would take our minds off my mom...."

Carrie's Secret

My head was spinning—Carrie hadn't come to my party because her mom was *drunk*?! "Oh, wow," I said. "I'm so sorry. I shouldn't have…I had no idea…I'm *really* sorry." It wasn't enough, but I didn't know what else to say.

We talked for over an hour. I found out that Carrie's life wasn't perfect at all. She didn't like to leave her mom alone at night, and she was afraid to bring people over, because she could never be absolutely sure her mom would be sober. Even her perfect clothes were hand-me-downs from her cousin. I'd thought she was a snob, but I hadn't really known her.

I spent a lot of time on IM that night, letting everyone know that I'd made up the rumor about Carrie because I was mad at her. Some of my friends got mad at *me*, and I had to apologize over and over. It was humiliating, but in the end I was glad I'd told the truth.

So you know what I learned from all this?

That you can't always tell what's going on in someone's life by what you see on the outside. And that you shouldn't judge people, because they might have good reasons for acting the way they do. And I think Carrie learned something, too—like that sometimes it's okay to tell people what's really going on in your life, even if it's really bad. After all, isn't that what friends are for?

ABOUT THE AUTHOR
Sarah, age 13, Conn.

I Toilet-Papered My Teacher's House

I **had some great teachers in sixth grade,** but I loved Mrs. Anderson* the most. She was young, pretty, funny, and she seemed to really like kids. We learned a lot in her class, but it was fun, too, partly because she was always making hysterical little comments—you just had to keep listening to see what she'd say next.

An Adored Teacher

I admired Mrs. Anderson so much, I was almost obsessed with her. I'm a good student and teachers have always liked me, but

All of the adults' names in this story have been changed.

I wanted Mrs. Anderson to think I was really special, just like I thought *she* was special. I even e-mailed her a few times, telling her how great I thought she was—and she answered me, too. I know teachers aren't supposed to have favorite students, but deep inside I was pretty sure I was one of hers.

The girls in my town are big on "rolling"— you know, covering someone's yard and

> We draped trees, bushes, and the lawn with long strips of toilet paper.

trees with toilet paper. We do it to people we like, and we don't mean anything bad by it. We mainly roll boys, but the year before we'd rolled Mrs. Gruber, our fifth-grade teacher, and she'd thought it was funny. So one Friday night, my friends Cammie and Madeline and I decided that it would be fun to roll Mrs. Anderson, too. It never even occurred to us that we might make our teacher mad—not funny, easygoing Mrs. Anderson!

My mom drove us to Mrs. Anderson's house, and we quickly got to work. We draped trees, bushes, and the lawn with long strips of toilet paper until everything looked amazing. As we were finishing up, the porch light came on, but we figured it was just one of those motion-activated lights. We ran for the car anyway, laughing and feeling on top of the world.

Back at Madeline's house, we left a message on Mrs. Anderson's voicemail, saying we'd rolled her. Then we called most of the kids in our class, too. Not realizing we'd already called her to "confess," a couple of the boys we'd talked to also called Mrs. Anderson's house—twice. The second time, Mr. Anderson answered, and he was not happy. He told the boys not to call there again, *ever*. They did, though, just a few minutes later, wanting to apologize to Mrs. Anderson herself.

Rolling...in Trouble?

A few minutes later, the phone rang at Madeline's house. It was Mrs. Anderson, and she was *furious*. We'd gone way too far, she

> How could something we'd done for fun turn out so wrong?

said, and she was upset that the boys kept calling. She was so mad she'd even called our principal, Dr. Breyer!

At that moment, I felt like the entire world had ended. I wanted to crawl in a box and never come out. The person that I had tried so hard to get to like me all of a sudden hated my guts. How could something we'd done for fun turn out so wrong?

I called my mom in tears. She felt terrible, too, since she was the one who'd driven us there. She tried to smooth things over by talking to Mrs. Anderson and Dr. Breyer. She explained to Mrs. Anderson that we'd only wanted to show her how much we loved her. Mrs. Anderson said that she understood that, but that *we* needed to understand that she and her husband had not taken it that way. She said that they were very big on keeping their work lives and personal lives separate, and she felt it was inappropriate for her students to have her phone number and address. Things went a little better with Dr. Breyer, at least. He said he understood where we were coming from, and that we wouldn't get into trouble.

I was still too worried about Mrs. Anderson to feel relieved about that, though. I cried all weekend, and my stomach was so tied up in knots that I couldn't eat. My parents tried to convince me that it would all blow over soon enough, but I *knew* I'd ruined everything. Mrs. Anderson would hold a grudge against me forever.

Scared and Misunderstood

On Monday, the sixth grade had an assembly about the rolling. Our names weren't mentioned, but the teachers explained that rolling was considered vandalism and could be a felony—a serious crime you can go to jail for! Cammie, Madeline, and I stared at the floor the whole time, too ashamed to look anyone in the eye. I was confused though, too. The teachers made it sound like we'd been *trying* to do something hurtful. I felt like no one understood, least of all Mrs. Anderson, the one person I cared most about.

I was so scared to face Mrs. Anderson again, but I also really wanted her to know how sorry I was. So after school, Cammie, Madeline, and I went to talk to her. Mrs. Anderson said she accepted our apology, but I thought she still seemed mad. I walked out of her classroom feeling heartbroken, still sure I was on her "bad" list forever.

I was wrong, though. Mrs. Anderson may have been upset about what we'd done, but she never held it

> I was so scared to face Mrs. Anderson again, but I also really wanted her to know how sorry I was.

against me. I guess she really *did* accept my apology, because after that day, she went right back to treating me the way she always had—like a student she really liked and cared about. I felt awkward around her at first, but as time went by, I started to believe that things really were okay between us.

So it turned out my parents were right,
even though I didn't believe them at the time: Life *does* go on. I realize now that not everyone sees things the way I do, and I've learned to think a little harder before I act. But most of all, I've learned that even if you make a huge mistake, people can forgive you, especially if you mean well and do your best to apologize. I sure don't plan to get in trouble again any time soon—and I definitely won't be rolling any more houses—but it *is* nice to find out that messing up isn't the end of the world.

ABOUT THE AUTHOR
Camille, age 11, La.

Chapter Eight

Living With Disabilities

I Am Not Stupid!

Have you ever really, really wanted to do **something,** but no matter how hard you tried, you just couldn't seem to get the hang of it? That's what learning to read was like for me.

When I was in kindergarten I loved books, so I couldn't wait to learn to read. I thought it would be so great to read my books all by myself.

I didn't have trouble at first, when we were just learning our letters—I was one of the best in my class. But by first grade, everyone caught up to me, and then they all passed me. They were all sounding out words, but I couldn't do it. Even though I tried hard, I just didn't get it.

Still, it wasn't too bad in first grade, because I wasn't the only one—other kids had trouble reading, too.

> I felt stupid, and I worried that maybe I'd *never* learn to read.

Also, the books were pretty simple, and I have a great memory, so I could get by. If I heard a story by someone like Dr. Seuss, I'd remember it so well I could "read" it if I had to. I even thought I was reading it, but I wasn't—I was just saying it from memory.

Then I got to second grade, and it got a lot harder. I still wasn't even reading at the kindergarten level. One day the teacher passed out copies of a book no one had seen before, and most of the other kids could read it, but I couldn't. Some of them were doing so well they were reading books like Harry Potter, but I was still stuck on Dr. Seuss. They'd say things like, "I can read that whole book in a minute, and you can't even read the first paragraph that fast." Or they'd ask me why I couldn't read something they thought was so easy. Even when they weren't trying to be mean, I'd feel terrible. I felt stupid, and I worried that maybe I'd *neve*r learn to read.

I was really frustrated, and so were my teacher and my mom. They thought I just wasn't trying hard enough, even though I was! My mom would sit with me while I did my homework, trying to help me with my spelling words and reading. Sometimes she would yell at me, or tell me I just needed to concentrate more, but it didn't help. No matter how hard I tried, I just couldn't get it. If I tried to sound out a word, I'd start off okay, and get the first couple of letters, but then I'd just make up the rest of the word. I'd look at a word like "good," and I'd get the "g" and the "o," but I'd think the word was "gosh," not "good." Sometimes, during silent reading time in school, I'd read a whole story like that. When I got to the end, it was as if I'd read a totally different story than everyone else!

The worst part was reading aloud in class. It was so embarrassing not being able to do something that most kids thought was easy. I'd take longer than everyone else, and I'd get all the words wrong. It was so bad that after a while the teacher stopped calling on me to read. In one way, that was a relief—but I also felt left out, and dumber than ever.

I was lucky, though, because even before I finished second grade, my mom and dad realized that something was wrong. They took me to a place called Lindamood-Bell, which has teachers who are trained to help kids like me. I had to take a bunch of tests, and afterward, they told my parents that I needed tutoring—classes with just me and a teacher—to help me catch up.

> It was so embarrassing not being able to do something that most kids thought was easy.

Getting Extra Help

I was scared to go to tutoring at first. I didn't want to leave my school and my friends. I didn't like being different from everyone else. I was nervous, too, because I thought even the teachers at Lindamood-Bell might not be able to help me. What if I was just too dumb to learn to read?

But much to my surprise, I *liked* being tutored! The teachers were so nice, and patient, too—no one ever got mad at me. I had five different teachers, and they all had lots of ways of explaining things. When I didn't get it one way, they'd explain it another way, and another, until I got it. It almost seemed like they tricked my brain into understanding how to sound out words. Finally—after a long time—everything just clicked in my brain, and I could read!

When I went back to my regular school,

everyone was amazed at how well I was reading. They even said that the school I'd gone to must be really good. I know now that I was never stupid—I just needed some extra help. And I'm really glad that I got it, too, because now reading is one of my favorite things to do!

ABOUT THE AUTHOR
Samantha, age 8, Calif.

Diabetes Changed My Whole Life

At the time, I was a perky, bright-eyed little kindergartner. I'd always been a skinny kid, but suddenly I was getting skinnier by the day. In two weeks, I lost seven pounds, and I was thirsty all the time, even though I kept drinking tons of water. On top of that, I had to pee every 45 minutes, even in the middle of the night. I felt like a slug.

My mom was shocked when the doctor said I had diabetes. She didn't think you could get diabetes unless someone else in your family had it, too. That's not true, though. Most people who get juvenile diabetes—the kind I have—don't have someone else in their family with the disease. No one knows for sure what causes juvenile diabetes. They do know that it's not caused by eating poorly or not taking care of yourself, though.

So what is diabetes? Everyone has an organ called a pancreas. The pancreas secretes something called insulin, which your body needs to turn the sugar in your food (even food that isn't really sweet, like milk and vegetables) into energy. When you have diabetes, your pancreas doesn't produce insulin. Without it, you can end up with too much sugar in your blood, which causes all sorts of problems and makes you feel really sick.

> My mom was shocked when the doctor said I had diabetes.

Because my body doesn't make any insulin, I have to take insulin every day to control my blood sugar. It's hard to know exactly how much insulin your body needs, though, because that changes depending on how much food is in your stomach, what you've eaten, how much exercise you've had, and other things, too. Without enough insulin, you get high blood sugar, which can make you go into a coma, have kidney failure, and even die. But if you get too much insulin, your blood sugar can go too low, and that's just as dangerous.

Finger Pricks, 10 Times a Day

To make sure I get the right amount of insulin, I have to check my blood sugar 8 to 10 times a day, including before I eat anything, or exercise, or go anywhere. I prick my finger and squeeze out a drop of blood onto a little machine called a glucometer. If my blood sugar is too high, I have to give myself insulin, and if it is too low, sugar.

> If my blood sugar goes too low, I feel dizzy and weak.

I used to get insulin from shots I would give myself. Now I have an insulin pump that is attached to a tube or "catheter," which is inserted in my body 24-7. I have to reinsert a new catheter in a different place in my stomach or hip at least every 72 hours, to prevent infection. The pump, which is about the size of a small cell phone, attaches to my shorts or skirt. The pump drips insulin into my body every three minutes, trying to act like a normal pancreas. I can also tell it to give me insulin whenever my blood sugar goes too high, or when I am eating. The pump makes my life easier, but it is not a cure.

Since the day of my diagnosis, I have pricked my fingers more than 16,000 times to test my blood sugar. I've had over 7,000 injections of insulin and 250 catheter insertions. If my blood sugar goes too low, I feel dizzy and weak. On the other hand, if my blood sugar goes too high, I get extremely thirsty and have to pee a lot. My childhood has been a physical and emotional roller coaster ride because of high and low blood sugar episodes. I never know how I'm going to feel during the day or night, and sometimes I go for days without feeling "good."

Being Different

Diabetes makes me different from other kids, and sometimes that's very hard. After I was diagnosed, my parents decided that it would be best for me to switch schools. On my first day at the new school, someone in my class spread a rumor that my diabetes was contagious! No one would even come near me, not even the girl who was supposed to show me around.

Probably the worst thing about having diabetes is worrying about what it might do to me. The disease can cause many complications, like kidney damage, blindness, heart disease…the list goes on and on. I used to think that if I took really good care of myself I wouldn't get complications, or that if I did, I would be grown before anything really bad happened. But I am already beginning to have kidney problems. I take medicine to help my kidneys, but there is no way to know if that will be enough. The thought of complications scares me really badly. I try not to think about it, but when I'm alone it is sometimes all I can think about.

What I Can Do...

I have learned some things from having diabetes, though. I know that I am responsible enough to take

> Diabetes also makes me "different" from other kids, and sometimes that's very hard.

care of my body. When I was in the third grade, I ended up in the hospital because my blood sugar got dangerously low when I was sleeping one night. (I had been very active the day before.) When I got home again, I vowed that from then on, I would control my diabetes instead of letting my diabetes control me. It is really hard work to keep my blood sugar at the right level, but I do everything I can to keep it balanced. It may not always work, but at least I am trying hard to keep it under control.

There is also some good that has come from me having diabetes, as strange as that sounds. I've discovered that I can do something to make a difference in the world. For several years, my family has worked to raise money for research to find a cure for diabetes. Also, last year I had the opportunity to testify before the U.S. Senate as a delegate to the Juvenile Diabetes Research Foundation Children's Congress. These experiences showed me that I do have a voice in our government, and that people are listening.

If I could stop having diabetes tomorrow, I'd jump at the chance. Every time I pass a fountain, I toss a penny in and wish for a cure. Every night I sit in bed and pray for a cure as long as I can stay awake. Until that day comes, though, I'll keep speaking out, and I'll keep working to raise money for research. That way, when there is a cure, I won't just be one of those who will benefit from it; I'll be one of the people who made it happen.

ABOUT THE AUTHOR
Caroline, age 11, Texas

Why Are Friendships So Confusing?

She knows everything about you...she'd never tell your secrets...she's your biggest fan. Who doesn't want a friend like that? **True friendship is a gift...** but it can be hard to find. Whether you're stuck in a fading friendship, caught in the popularity trap, or dealing with mean girls, we'll break down **the solutions** to your problems step by step. Best of all, we'll teach you how to **free yourself from poisonous friendships forever** and be the best friend you can be. Soon, you'll be meeting new people and making friends who truly respect and understand you...because **you deserve first-rate friendships.**

Getting Unstuck

Remember when you got up the courage to tell your crush you liked him...and found out he didn't like you back? Didn't you wish you knew someone who had **all the answers?** Well, have no fear! Not only do we know exactly how to handle your crush (what is wrong with him, anyway?), but we also know **how to deal** with a **gazillion** other sticky situations. Like when your BFF blabs your deepest secret to the entire school...or when you make a total fool of yourself onstage. We'll also tell you how to handle being cornered by a mean dog...or stranded at the mall...and much, much more! By the last page, **you'll be ready to deal with anything!**

Drama, Drama, Drama

Stuck between friends? Tired of your sibs?
Self-conscious about your body? Crushing big time?
You're not alone. Every month, girls write to Discovery
Girls magazine to ask Ali, our **advice** columnist, for **help
with issues** like these. When it comes to girls' most
troublesome questions, Ali has all the answers you need.
Here, she tackles your questions on everything from family
to friendship to school to boys...and much, much more. No
matter what you're going through, **you'll find answers
to your problems inside.** Ali is here to help!